FESTIVAL OF FAVOUR

WHY am I here, WHAT is expected of me, and WHERE am I headed when this life is over?

By
Oluwaseun Opadokun

Published by
S.P.O.T.S Publishing
www.festivaloffavour.co.uk

First Edition
ISBN - 978-1-8380988-0-3 – Ebook
ISBN - 978-1-8380988-1-0 – Paperback

Printed
In the United Kingdom and the United States of America

To request Oluwaseun for speaking engagements, or interviews, please send an email to:
oluwaseunopadokun@festivaloffavour.co.uk

Oluwaseun's books are available at special discounts when purchased in bulk for promotions or as donations for educational and training purposes.

Limit of Liability/Disclaimer of Warranty

This publication is designed to provide accurate and authoritative information in regard to the subject matter covered. It is sold with the understanding that the publisher and author are not engaged in rendering physiological, financial, legal or other licensed services. The publisher and the author make no representations or warranties with respect to the completeness of the contents of this work. If expert assistance or counselling is needed, the services of a specific professional should be sought. Neither the publisher nor the author shall be liable for damages arising here from. The fact that an organisation or website is referred to in this work as a citation and/or a potential source of further information does not mean that the author or the publisher endorses the information that the organisation or website may provide or recommendations it may make, nor does the cited organisation endorse affiliation of any sort to this publication. Also, readers should be aware that due to the ever-changing information from the web, Internet websites and URLs listed in this work may have changed or been removed.

All trademarks or names referenced in this book are the property of their respective owners, and the publisher and author are not associated with any product or vendor mentioned.

DEDICATION

This book is dedicated to the Almighty God, who has made my life a blessing, thanks to his gift of an amazing wife Titilayomi and the three amazing children He has given us – Oluwapelumi, Oluwatitofunmi and Oluwasikemi.

ACKNOWLEDGEMENTS

For all of you who have picked up this book, this is the best place to start; the lessons actually start from here.

I will not pretend to be a writer or claim to be an expert on world affairs. I am just an ordinary family guy, blessed by an extraordinary God and empowered by that same extraordinary God to do exploits. This means that whatever response you may want to accord the contents of this book should go to the One who empowered and inspired its contents.

I am grateful to God for counting me worthy to be a vessel He sees fit to use. One major lesson God has taught me is that there is no room for self-will or self-glory when it comes to Him. He determines the how, when and where. All I can do is make myself available, emptying myself of all that is me, and allowing the God who does exploits with the most unworthy of vessels to take all the glory through me.

I thank God for my parents, Deacon and Deaconess Opadokun. You showed me the path of life, and I thank God both of you are still walking the path. I thank my in-laws, Daddy and Mummy Olaoti for trusting your daughter to this starry-eyed boy all those years ago. I appreciate my uncles and aunties, in particular Uncle Ayo Opadokun and wife, who opened their home to me so many years ago. I pray I can learn from your hearts of selfless service. My uncle, ASP (rtd.) Remi

Opadokun and family, thank you for being supporting us all these years.

I appreciate my sisters, Dr. Mrs. Showunmi and Mrs. Oshilesi, your husbands and children too. Uncle Niyi Oyelade and family, I appreciate the impact your lives have made on mine. My own family – the very extended Opadokun family (Bola, Tunde, Kayode, Olayiwola and sisters, Baruwas, the Olaoti boys (Gbenga and Sunkanmi), the Dadas; may we all be worthy of heaven.

I appreciate all who have made spiritual impact in my life – the families of Revd. & Mrs. Odewale, Revd. & Mrs. Mojolagbe, Revd. Dr. & Mrs. Ogunbode, Revd. Dr. & Mrs. Adetutu, members of Bethel Baptist Church Ilorin, Nigeria, the Diaconate, Youth fellowship, Sunday School and Ushering departments of Ikate Baptist Church.

I appreciate Pastor Yemisi Folaju and the RCCG Vine Branch parish (UK) family, as well as Pastors Ayo & Yinka Ayeni, Pastor & Pastor Mrs. Ojo, Pastor & Mrs. Babalola, Pastor Femi Dina, and the entire leadership team and members of the RCCG Croydon Tabernacle (UK).

I also appreciate the invaluable contribution of Victor Kwegyir and the Vike Springs Publishing Ltd. team; may the Lord shine His light upon your ways and grant you His inimitable favour.

I acknowledge the impact of the First Bank of Nigeria Group Compliance family and the opportunity given me to serve in various capacities. The bosses I have been privileged to work with in the past – Mr. Lucky Esekhaigbe, Mr. Ibukun Olomo, Mrs. Pamela Nwokolo, Mr. Uduak Nelson Udoh, Mrs. Adeyemi Ogunmoyela and Mrs. Olapeju Oluwajana; I appreciate God's touch on your life, may we all be worthy of heaven. His time of favour is here.

CONTENTS

INTRODUCTION

WHY FESTIVAL OF FAVOUR?

In my private and quiet moments, I have asked myself just what the motivation for this book was. So many things have crossed my mind at various times, but one thing that has remained constant is this: God wants something extraordinary for my life. He spent time creating me and then equipping me with the necessary skills and talents necessary for fulfilling His purpose for me. Then He placed me in a particular place for a particular time for a particular purpose, so I could give back to my generation all that God has placed in me. How then do I discover these skills and how do I develop them? How do I know what I am created for? I have read many books and heard many sermons on this, so I will not bother repeating all I have heard because I must have forgotten some of them already. I just want to share with you what God has taught me over the years and how He has helped me apply myself to the lessons He is teaching me through my daily experiences. This is therefore not an attempt to bamboozle anyone with a wealth of words but rather to share the wealth of God's Word, and how it has helped make sense of my life's experiences so far.

This book is therefore not another book of Revelations; only one needs to be written and it has already been. This small book will start at the beginning: Who am I and what am I doing here on earth? How do I know how and where I fit into this complex conundrum called earth? Do I qualify to enjoy God's favour? If I do, how do I enjoy it? How do I discover direction from the right source and how do I change my focus if I am on the wrong track? What is in this journey of discovery for me and how will I know when I have arrived? View this book as a discovery or an eye-opener. It cannot really answer all of life's questions; only God can. It can only show you the way to find God and His purpose for your life. Don't take its contents as the gospel truth; only the Bible is true. God intends for my life to be a continual feast, with a constant flow of His favour in my direction. It is my duty to discover what my role on earth is. Nobody will do it for me. It's a personal thing; a personal working out and a personal gain.

Join me on this journey as we both discover why we are who we are and what God has put in us that the world is waiting in earnest expectation for.

Throughout this book, our journey of discovery will centre on these four issues:

1. Who am I – questions on identity and endowment

2. What am I here for – question of eternity in the past, present and future

3. Where am I supposed to occupy – questions on location, pursuit, purpose and direction

4. Who am I to go with - questions on friendship, impact, relationships, timing and eternity

The connecting theme is the title of this book, as we respond to God's invitation to join Him at work.

Bible References are from the following versions:
GNB – Good News Bible
KJV – King James Version
NIV – New International Version
ESV – English Standard Version
NLT – New Living Translation

CHAPTER 1

WHO AM I AND WHAT AM I ON EARTH FOR?

In him we were also chosen, having been predestined according to the plan of him who works out everything in conformity with the purpose of his will. – Ephesians 1:11 NIV

I once watched a movie in which Jackie Chan had been involved in an accident and had lost his memory. He had quite a number of unpleasant experiences and then, at one point, he left everyone, climbed up a hill and screamed to the entire world: "**Who am I?**" This is a question we all must ask and find concrete answers to if our lives are to make sense and make an impact. The heading of this chapter, although in two parts, really gets answered as a whole, because if you know who you really are, then you can get busy and productive at the very purpose of your being and existence. The questions will be answered not in any particular order but like a puzzle with many pieces all leading to a beautiful conclusion.

I believe that every soul who is alive presently – whether consciously or unconsciously – has a purpose ordained by God. Picture this: nobody makes a product without first having an idea of what it is supposed to do. The idea may be in its conceptual stage, awaiting perfection and processing, but there must be a clear idea of the direction the product is to take. Whether the product then achieves its pre-production hype is a different story altogether, but what is important to note is this: there is a purpose to everything created. How then can we think that God could make a whole human being and not have a plan for him? Can God really create 7.1 billion directionless, purposeless, clueless people and just place them in the space called earth? One thing is certain: our progression from travelling by foot to travelling by air and our degeneration from fighting with mere fists to shooting down whole cities with atomic and nuclear weapons show how far man has come on his journey of discovery of purpose.

For we are His workmanship, created in Christ Jesus unto good works, which God hath before ordained that we should walk in them. - Eph. 2:10 KJV

Our lives are more than mere accidents; God must mean more than what we have or are presently. The passage above says we are His workmanship, His masterpieces. We are an ongoing project, a work-in-progress, a never-ending wonder. No wonder man is the most complex of all of God's creation. So many theories have been expounded as to the origin of man that it is difficult for any mortal man not to really wonder who he or she really is. In this complex structure called earth, I think we owe it to God and to our family to really discover who we really are and where we fit. The passage also says God had prepared good works for us to do, long before we were even born. That is some deep stuff. Long before I became mature, aware or even conscious of who I am, the owner of my life already laid out a path before me. He drew up a manual and a course of action for my life. My life is part of the complex, intricate design called earth and I must find that path, that course and that plan if I am to make an impact the way God has ordained for me.

So many people pass through earth making some kind of impact. I do not think there is anyone alive who does not make some kind of impact. We hear of people who have made a great impact on humanity and think that indeed, they must have fulfilled their purpose. We hear of our own late MKO Abiola of Nigeria, the late Nelson Mandela of South Africa, the late Kwame Nkrumah of Ghana, among many others. Yet, shockingly, if these people were still alive, some of them may wish they could rewrite parts of their lives and live it in a different way. *Purpose* isn't what the world celebrates; it's what God –the giver of purpose – says it is that matters. May I not get to heaven and discover that I wasted my life living for other people, leaving my own purpose undiscovered and unfulfilled. Fortunately, it is never too late to discover purpose; only the dead have left it too late. As long as I'm alive, the journey is mine to undertake.

But now thus saith the Lord that created thee, O Jacob, and he that formed thee, O Israel. Fear Not, for I have redeemed thee, I have called thee by thy name; thou art mine. - Isaiah 43:1 KJV

Indeed, the journey cannot be understood without first establishing who we are and whose we are. In a world of over seven billion people from over a hundred countries on seven continents, there must be a struggle for identity and space. We want our lives to mean something; to make an impact. I think the journey must start from an understanding of our identity and origin. It helps to know where we are coming from so we can know if we are on the right track as we journey on. All the passages quoted so far underline a simple fact: our lives are not our own. That simple fact is the biggest problem we face in a world where there seems to be a competition as to who is the smartest and the best. The world seems to be a racecourse and we all are athletes competing for an unknown prize. We don't know what it is, yet we all run, pursuing the enigma called SUCCESS, not even sure what it means and not even certain if and when we attain it. We are constantly bombarded with the image of success on TV, people telling us how our lives are to be defined by certain standards. We forget one simple fact: our lives are not our own. Is it possible for a Samsung television to turn around and tell its maker that it wants to function as a Yamaha power generating set?

The Bible says in Isaiah 29:16b KJV "**or shall the thing framed say of him that framed it, He had**

no understanding?" God must be feeling a little let down when we allow things He created to tell us how and when our lives should have meaning, instead of allowing the creator Himself to dictate the terms of our lives. We must go back to basics and let the standard-bearer be the only standard we look up to. Until we get it right, our lives can never be right. You may also wonder how possible it is for your life to make sense in the multitude of people who inhabit the earth. If the earth's resources couldn't sustain all of us, I believe God would not have created all of us. His resources are limitless and His knowledge unfathomable, which leads us to the discovery in Isaiah 43:1 KJV, above that God knows me by my name.

I pause here and consider what I have just written: "He calls me by my name." He knows me so intimately that He can call me by name. He says I am His. If nothing else makes sense, this sure does. The creator of the complex universe calls a mere mortal man like myself by name. This tells me I'm of a special stock to God, I'm not ordinary and I cannot live an ordinary existence. I have a big price on my head, because I belong to the creator of the whole world. Before this gets more complex, let me ask you: what is your name? What are you called? Who or what determines your identity? I believe this is the starting point. If I do not know myself or if I cannot find myself in God, how do I even begin to understand what my life is all about? Myles Munroe once said: "When purpose is unknown, abuse is inevitable." If I'm still struggling to find myself, I'm not sure I can be convinced God cares about me. If I have not run to God, I will keep running an endless race. Only in God can I find rest to be what He wants me to be at the time He wants me to be it. When I have settled the question of my identity in God, then can I be free of the world's expectations and ever-shifting standards.

The question still remains: Who am I? Have I found my niche? Do I even know my name, so that when God calls me, I can answer? Am I still struggling to catch my breath under the burden of expectations from family, friends, peers and colleagues? None of these questions can be answered outside of God. That is the summary of our origins. You cannot catch your breath outside of the God who breathed into you and gave you life. Try anything: politics, possessions, power, privilege and position. If you seek them outside of God, you will keep running out of breath, because it is only in God who gives life that you can be sustained. You can live to be 120 years old, but if God is not involved, your life may just remain just a life once lived; nothing else.

Let me summarise all I have said in these few words: outside of God, there is no purpose, direction or plan. You don't buy a brand-new product and throw away the manual. You would be lost without it. It's the same with our lives. The journey of discovery starts at the feet of He who holds the course, distance and travel plans. If you want to journey well and arrive safely, you must get the plans from God. He alone knows where and how our lives are to make sense and we must go to Him before we face the world. If we get the order wrong, the world will beat us silly and lead us astray, but if we seek God first before seeking to change the world, the world will know there is something different about us because we dance to a different tune and live a different life from its standards.

The word which came to Jeremiah from the Lord, saying, Arise, and go down to the potter's house, and there I will cause thee to hear my words. Then I went down to the potter's house, and, behold, he wrought a work on the wheels. And the vessel that he made of clay was marred in the hand of the potter: so he made it again another vessel, as seemed good to the potter to make it. Then the word of the Lord came to me, saying, O house of Israel, cannot I do with you as this potter? saith the Lord. Behold, as the clay is in the potter's hand, so are ye in mine hand, O house of Israel. - Jeremiah 18:1- 6 KJV

Some key lessons jump out in the verses above:

1. The potter sits as the ultimate decider of what happens to the clay.

2. The potter can also change his mind on the final purpose of the clay.

3. The reasons for the change in purpose is left to the potter to determine, and he does not have to answer to anyone.

4. The clay must be a willing and silent participant in its processing into the finished product.

Now, let us break these four points down further and apply them to our lives.

Firstly, at no time does God call a conference to decide what to do with us or we are to appear. He sits as the controller of the universe, deciding our origin, parentage, skin colour, skin texture, facial patterns, DNA, gifting and several other things. Furthermore, God does not run a consultancy service; He is the boss and the king of all. He works on us, shaping, moulding, melting, filling and beating fine until we are exactly what He has in mind. While He is in the process of fashioning us, a lot may happen. God still reserves the right to decide what He wants us to be. God is not fickle-minded, unsure of what He wants, but will take time and pay careful attention to the details of our lives so we can turn out to be what He has created us to be. Whatever the reasons God has for His decisions, the best is His ultimate desire.

Notice that in all the above, the clay is silent. I do not recall at any time seeing clay dictate how best it wants to be used or where it thinks its gifts are best applied. I am yet to see a clay product compare itself to other clay products or any other product for that matter. In any case, clay was not made with a mouth, so it cannot speak, and there will be no basis of comparison with other products, because they are not all of the same stock.

If only we could comprehend this concept as human beings. How did we ever think we had a say in the matter or that we knew more than the God who created and formed us as He saw fit? How did we ever come to the conclusion that we could dictate our area and scope of influence? We have suddenly grown "mature" thinking we know what is best for us. We tell God we do not like how we look or where He has placed us or the gifts that we possess; we think we know better. The story of the potter and the clay teaches a great lesson – impact and purpose is not determined by the created but by the creator. Purpose is not the business of created clay; it is the business of God the potter. He creates, fills, equips, places and strengthens. The clay just has to cooperate and it will experience the glory that accompanies a purpose-driven existence.

Closely linked to the understanding of identity is the issue of ownership. In fact, you cannot discuss identity without ownership. Back to the Garden of Eden, **Genesis 1:26 – 27; 2:7 KJV** establish the concept of identity and ownership. When God created man in the Garden, His mark of identity and ownership was placed on man. God created man from a perfect template, in His image, to reflect His power and nature. Man belonged to God and was to represent God in all things. His seal of ownership was the breath of God put into man's nostrils. Without the breath, he remained just dust.

Why is the concept of identity and ownership so important to this journey of discovery? If we search through Scriptures, you will discover a fundamental truth about God – He is a God who lays claim to whatever belongs to Him, and He has a bounden duty to protect and preserve whatever He owns. Come with me as we check out a few verses, as we seek to gain a fundamental understanding of the importance of ownership and identity.

The earth is the Lord's, and the fullness thereof; the world, and they that dwelleth therein. – Psalm 24:1 KJV

This verse establishes the truth of the creation account as recorded in Genesis. Everything we can see, touch, hear, feel or perceive belongs to God. Now, that is a fundamental statement. If all I can see belongs to God, it means that an accounting will be done to God on all I have taken and used from His creation. If I know that everything I hold is held temporarily and as a trust of which an account will be demanded; I will watch my actions, my motives and my intentions. **So then every one of us shall give account of himself to God. – Romans 14:12 KJV**

How could I accept that God owns the entire world as we know it, and then deny His ownership of the breath that makes me human? How could I accept that God is in charge of the world, and then live as if I answer to nobody except myself? The world seems to have lost its awe and awareness of God. We now have a world without direction, order or fear of God. We take life we cannot create; we create things that will destroy life; we decimate God's creation – sometimes for sport – in order to satisfy a hunger for something deep in us that is crying to be filled. We fill our lives with causes and activities, excluding God, the real owner of the life.

The heavens are thine, the earth also is thine: as for the world and the fulness thereof, thou hast founded them. - Psalm 89:11 KJV

Gilead is mine, and Manasseh is mine; Ephraim also is the strength of mine head; Judah is my lawgiver – Psalm 60:7 KJV

For every beast of the forest is mine, and the cattle upon a thousand hills – Psalm 50:10 KJV

The silver is mine, and the gold is mine, saith the Lord of hosts. - Haggai 2:8 KJV

You really cannot argue with God's claim of ownership over all of creation. Which of us was there when the foundations of the earth were laid? Where are the foundations established? Who will take anything away from His hands unless He lets go? Understanding this is key to the hunger to know more about this God and to seek Him out.

But who am I, and what is my people, that we should be able to offer so willingly after this sort? For all things come of thee, and of thine own have we given thee. – 1 Chron 29:14 KJV

A clear understanding of who we are and whose we are is key to how we live our lives. David had a fundamental understanding of the proper order – we must first understand who and whose we are, before we can fully appreciate the place of possessions and position in our lives.

Behold, all souls are mine; as the soul of the father, so also the soul of the son is mine: the soul that sinneth, it shall die. – Ezekiel 18:4 KJV

God leaves us in no doubt as to His claim over all of creation: the passages quoted above all testify of God's claim of ownership. If the verses are true, and we accept what they say as the gospel truth, then a decision must be made: are we going to accept this Truth or are we going to hold on to convenient deceit? Will my life reflect God as the real owner of my life or am I still struggling to accept the authority of God over my life?

The final verse for review here is **Isaiah 1:2 -3 KJV: Hear, O heavens, and give ear, O earth: for the Lord hath spoken, I have nourished and brought up children, and they have rebelled against me. The ox knoweth his owner, and the ass his master's crib: but Israel doth not know, my people doth not consider**.

Isn't it sad to consider where man is at this point in time? Long before man was ever made, the provision for his sustenance and nourishment had been put in place. God spent five and a half days creating all other things man would need. Man was then created and placed in the midst of abundance and plenty, only required to keep the garden, tend it, and live his life in peace. Fast forward a few years, and it appears man has come full circle. God went on record to say he regretted he ever made man, because his thoughts were continually wicked.

Through the generations following, even with the ones He chose for Himself and lavished so many blessings on, the refrain was the same – rejection of God and a denial of His ownership and control of their lives. In Isaiah, there is a sad testament to the continual rejection and denial of God as the owner and controller of our lives. We hear God calling the heavens and the earth as witnesses to His people's rejection of Him. He had nourished and fed them, He had brought them up as His own children, yet they had rebelled against Him and rejected His Lordship.

Even animals know their owners and where they are to sleep for the night, but for us, it is a continuous cycle of pain in God's heart as we live our lives, deliberately ignoring His claim of ownership of our lives. It is a wonder we keep asking why the world is the way it is. When the clay starts to question the wisdom and authority of the potter, the unnatural is bound to happen. When the created thinks it knows more about itself than the creator, there is a problem. The state of the world today cannot be any other way, because the created has told the Creator to keep off.

If I acknowledge this truth about ownership, how dare I live as though I own my life? How could I ever imagine that I answer to nobody except myself? If I know that God can withdraw His breath from me at any time, and that He has made me the way I am so I can bring Him glory, I will live my life responsibly and with a sense of accountability. **Moreover it is required in stewards, that a man be found faithful – 1 Corinthians 4:2 KJV.**

Let me also pause here and ask – have you discovered your identity? Do you know who you are? Do you know who you belong to and in whose hands the reins of your life are? I know many of us will claim that God is the one in charge of our lives, but what I do know is the fruits of your life will reveal the identity of the person who is truly in charge. When what your life produces causes men to ask again who you are, you need to check your life and be sure you are owned right.

Now that we seem to have established who we are, how do we know what we are on earth for? How do we make that all-important discovery? How do we go from knowing to doing? One of life's greatest tragedies is that the world places so much emphasis on head-knowledge and not much on heart-knowledge. We have so many doctorate degree holders and professors of amazing specialities who do not even know or acknowledge that there is a God. All they accept is that there is a cosmic force that holds the world in place or that a big bang occurred and the world was formed. Some even teach that we evolved from maggots or apes. It's difficult to imagine that a so-called learned person saying man evolved from apes. Head-knowledge is good if it leads to a deeper understanding of who God is. It makes no sense if it leads you away from your true origins and sinks you into the pool of misdirected and misguided "knowledge". Are you pursuing head-knowledge or heart-knowledge?

The testimony is this: God has given us eternal life, and this life has its source in his Son. Whoever has the Son has this life; whoever does not have the Son of God does not have life. - 1 John 5:11-12 GNB

For his invisible attributes, namely, his eternal power and divine nature, have been clearly perceived, ever since the creation of the world, in the things that have been made. So they are without excuse -Romans 1:20 ESV

God has indeed made His priorities clear. He has determined the source, nature and power of the knowledge He desires us to have. That knowledge is the type that brings and gives life and it is only received through His son. All our accomplishments, achievements and acquisitions must go through Him for them to make sense, otherwise we run the risk of pursuing lifeless dead-ends. Everything God has done or said in His word is tailored towards helping us see ourselves as God sees us. His entire purpose for creating us has been established in His Word and only by careful study and diligent application of its contents can our lives make sense. Forget the drama the television screens give you; a life lived outside of God's purpose and direction will literally end up in flames.

The Bible lays down the terms of the search and the conditions to be met in order to earn the rewards. The rewards too are spelt out in clear terms, so that we all know beforehand what we are getting into. You will not get halfway through and claim that nobody told you that it would be this hard. You must count the cost.

GETTING TO KNOW GOD

After the earthquake came a fire, but the Lord was not in the fire. And after the fire came a gentle whisper. When Elijah heard it, he pulled his cloak over his face and went out and stood at the mouth of the cave. – 1 Kings 19:12-13 NIV

We like effects – earthquakes, fire and wind. Unfortunately, noise doesn't guarantee God's presence. Many things happening in the world today make the hearts of men tremble, but God wants our hearts to seek out His voice. His voice was what created the earth as we see it now and His voice is what Elijah heard and made him tremble. What moves you – unpredictable world events, the economy or the certainty of God's written and spoken Word?

I have heard of various job functions in different companies and one of the most complex and intriguing is that of a risk analyst in an insurance company. What the guy is expected to do is to measure the exposure the company would have if it had to sell insurance policies to various classes of people. He has to consider the age, drinking, eating and smoking habits, marital, financial, emotional and psychological profiles of prospective customers before collecting premiums from them. Yet, with all the money and time spent "analysing", things still go horribly wrong.

What then is amiss? Nobody can know more about another person more than the God who created and equipped him, and nobody can determine what will go wrong for any person more than the God who holds the life manual in His hands.

We run from pillar to post, from financial expert to psychologist, expecting them to correctly diagnose what is wrong with our lives. We even seek out "men of God", somehow hoping, like Naaman, that they will somehow tell us what is wrong with us and how we can fix ourselves. While I do not doubt God's ability to use any man to help us, one lesson I have learnt is that no other man can experience God on your behalf. You can either seek Him out by yourself or spend your entire life wondering why God keeps using that other man while you are left holding your head in regret.

Regrettably, we also forget that men of God are men first of all, and will never become God. They are human, weak and mortal and it is God who makes them who and what they are. If you want to know why you are here on earth, why not go straight to the source?

Hear the word of the Lord, O children of Israel, for The Lord has a controversy with the inhabitants of the land. There is no faithfulness or steadfast love, and no knowledge of God in the land; there is swearing, lying, murder, stealing, and committing adultery; they break all bounds, and bloodshed follows bloodshed.

Therefore the land mourns, and all who dwell in it languish, and also the beasts of the field and

the birds of the heavens and even the fish of the sea are taken away. Yet let no one contend, and let none accuse, for with you is my contention, O priest. You shall stumble by day, the prophet also shall stumble with you by night; and I will destroy your mother.

My people are destroyed for lack of knowledge; because you have rejected knowledge, I reject you from being a priest to me. And since you have forgotten the law of your God, I also will forget your children. - Hosea 4:1-6 ESV

A fairly long passage, but one that encapsulates the importance and necessity of acquiring the right knowledge and the importance of getting the source right. Israel knew all the laws in the Old Testament, they could recite them by rote. Yet their daily lives were in contrast with what their mouths professed. The commandments read: thou shall not kill, thou shall not commit adultery, thou shall not bear false witness; yet they could not comply because they did not have the inner knowledge that could help. That is what is wrong with the world today: a lot of knowledge, but so little of the right kind; so many discoveries, yet so much emptiness and busyness, because there is a void in each life that only the creator of that life can fill, and until God fills it, man will only keep running, without knowing why he is running, what is pursuing him, or what he really wants. We now have museums celebrating how far man has come in his journey of discovery and knowledge, but nothing can fully contain the treasures that accrue to a man who has the right kind of knowledge.

In all of these words, something strikes me. God craves a relationship with man. Sounds funny? God, the author of the universe, the connecting thread holding all the pieces and puzzles of this universe together, the One who calls the whole earth – amazing as it is – his mere footstool, wants to have a relationship with me? Sounds odd but then read this: **For by him were all things created, that are in heaven, and that are in earth, visible and invisible, whether they be thrones, or dominions, or principalities, or powers: all things were created by him, and for him. - Colossians 1:16 KJV** Note the last sentence here: ALL things were created by Him and for Him. If something is made for me, it has to give me pleasure. If God made me for Himself, how could I think I could ever amount to anything outside of Him?

For in him we live, and move, and have our being; as certain also of your own poets have said, For we are also his offspring. - Acts 17:28 KJV If I am God's offspring, and have my being in Him, then nothing I do outside of Him will ever give me the peace I need. I was created to give God pleasure and to replicate His attributes in my life. After all, as His offspring, I must show attributes of my father. If I must fulfil my father's purpose for making me, I must seek out His ideas, plans and desires for my life. I cannot afford to leave such momentous decisions in the hands of created men like myself, who will also have to answer to our common creator as to whether the journey they undertook was self-inflicted or God-directed. I must seek the Lord for myself.

The verse before the one just quoted in the paragraph above says: **That they should seek the Lord, if haply they might feel after him, and find him, though he be not far from every one of us. - Acts 17:27 KJV** I owe it to myself. The danger is that everything has a time frame; nobody is promised eternity this side of heaven. We were only promised eternity on the other side of this present life and the things we do now are the preparations for that eternity. We are here for a limited time only and we must work within the timeframe allotted to us. **Seek ye the Lord while he may be found, call ye upon him while he is near. - Isaiah 55:6 KJV**

Where then is God to be found in all of these confounding and confusing state of affairs? Can I really find God in the midst of the most distressing of circumstances? Yes you can. In fact, because you cannot succeed at anything outside of Him, everything must start with Him.

Just as it has been established, God is near to all who call on Him. That is it – **those who call on Him**. One thing I have learned as a Christian is that we talk a lot about all the Christian graces and practices – fasting, prayer, Bible study, fellowship, communion and the like. We know what they entail but we do not KNOW how they practically work. We are experts at reading about them but novices at living them out. We know a lot about them but our hearts cannot fully comprehend their requirements in practical terms.

I once lived in a neighbourhood where full-grown women would come to a stream of water close to where we lived. A young man was the "pastor" there, bathing them and "fasting and praying" on their behalf to ward off evil. These women didn't know that evil had already come to stay and that only a personal knowledge of the One who created them and knows them intimately could deliver them from evil. People, only God knows us so intimately that nothing escapes His attention. As you make a conscious decision to seek God, you will discover that He is very near to you and craves a relationship with you.

How then do I seek Him? How do I know when I have found Him? I'm sure a few people will expect some magical, complex answer. You can only find Him through his manual – the Bible. Sounds simple? Yes, a book written by ordinary men but inspired by an extraordinary God holds the answer to all of life's questions and reveals the secrets of God to all who will seek them out. I have read books on self-discovery and positive thinking; I have sat down to listen to men talk about things that made impact on their lives.

But I have also listened to testimonies of men who have encountered the power in the Word. I came away with the conviction that the only permanent, long-lasting change that man needs is that which only the Word can provide. I have seen gun-toting rogues become Bible-wielding evangelists; I have seen prostitutes become Godly mothers, all because they encountered the power of the Word. Nothing else can bring that change, no matter how solid its theories and principles are. I love the passage that says: **For the word of God is quick, and powerful, and sharper than any two-edged sword, piercing even to the dividing asunder of soul and spirit, and of the joints and marrow, and is a discerner of the thoughts and intents of the heart. - Hebrews 4:12 KJV**

Nothing can stand in the way of the sweeping, purging effects of God's Word. Before it, hearts and motives are revealed and made plain. What that verse also establishes is that to every life, there must be a personal encounter. I agree that the lessons a man has learnt from the impact of the Word of God on his life can help you, but you cannot live your life fully only on the experiences of other people. I cannot run from one church to another ministry, seeking that awesome experience, without seeking out the God that gives the experience Himself.

Check out the story of Elijah in 1 Kings 19 quoted above again: another similar tragedy is the assumption that the way He worked with Elijah is the way He must work with me. Elijah assumed that because he was the visible prophet of God, there was no one left who could do what he was doing. God taught him a few lessons but just two will suffice here: firstly, never assume that God needs you to do the work He wants to get done. He can use anything and anybody to pass His message across. The fact that you are at work for God does not make you irreplaceable; the sense of responsibility should keep you eternally dependent on God for sustenance and impact.

Secondly, there are different experiences God will bring your way to help you know Him intimately. Elijah experienced the wind, the fire and the earthquake, but the Bible records that God was not in any of them. God chose not to speak to Elijah through those means because He wanted to teach Elijah not to be moved by the physical, the emotional or the special effects around him. God could have spoken through the effects; after all, Moses experienced God through the burning bush, God's judgement was spoken against Korah, Dathan and Abiram via an earthquake when they rebelled against God, and the mighty rushing wind heralded the coming of the Holy Spirit at Pentecost. Who says God is limited in impact and effects?

By now, you know that God is everywhere and fills all things in all ways. He decides how to reach a man at the time He pleases and in the manner He chooses. Never limit God to the level of your intellect; never assume to know how God would speak in a particular situation. Do not be so dependent on what a man says that what God says makes no impact. If God can create over seven billion people with peculiar fingerprints, I am sure He can speak to all of them in different ways without repeating any method. It is a sign of ignorance to ever think that you have got God figured out.

I then must make a choice: do I go to God for guidance or do I seek out the regular tokens of liars?

Do I allow the Word of God do His work or do I allow my heart to follow after vain dissipations? I have a choice to make: go with God or go with the devil; make peace with God or keep running. If God created me to give Him pleasure, it then means I cannot be doing something I hate to do if it is His will for my life. If I have discovered His purpose for my life, life ceases to be pain or pressure but waking up becomes a pleasure, as it is another opportunity to influence lives for God.

Have I gone to God for His blueprint for my life? Am I pursuing matters close to God's heart for my life? Do I know what He wants me to do or what my life's course entails? Until I know that with a deep conviction that no circumstance can shake, then my journey has not started. Fortunately, it is never too early or too late to seek out God's direction for my life. The parable of the hired servants is on point here. Many were recruited at the start of the day, some at the sixth hour, and some at the ninth hour. They all got the same reward, the same wages. That's God – fair to the point of showing unusual favour; a God who does not regard time, circumstances or privilege when he chooses to bless people who seek Him.

For every question that may arise across the spectrum of life from birth to death, answers are provided in the Word of God. From dealing with the origins of life to issues of sexual purity, the purity of love and the futility of infatuation and the controversial question of divorce, all are answered adequately in the Word of God. The Bible is the manual of life, the constitution of our being, existence and well-being. Follow its teachings and you will discover a deep well of wealth and prosperity. One warning though – you can never understand its contents without the help of its author. Many self-help gadgets and theories exist on the Internet, but for the Bible, you just can't help yourself to the deep secrets and mysteries of its pages. You need the help of the Holy Spirit to unlock the secrets.

At this point, I need to clarify one thing. The preceding paragraph assumes that the person reading this is born again, in the proper sense of the word as God established it in John 3, not the pretentious and superficial thing people mockingly call it these days. We now hear of born-again drunkards who now drink less than they did before or smokers who now smoke less than they used to before. I am referring to the deep, surgical operation that the Holy Spirit does in the heart of man, dealing with the self that is prone to sin and giving man the strength to live in accordance with the dictates of the Word of God. It's being born of the Spirit and having that "seal of redemption" that is a deposit of God in a man's life and a guarantee that when this present life ends, the real life starts with God in the New Jerusalem.

It is being able to make a distinction between what your old life represented and what God is presently doing in your life. If you really cannot see a difference between the two contrasting lifestyles, then check your connection. Too often, we become used to "church". Many of us were born in church and forced to attend weekly programmes. In the Baptist church, there was the Sunbeam Band for children between 09 years, Girls' Auxillary for girls between 10 -19 and the Royal Ambassadors for young boys of 10-25 or till they were married. There was the Lydia Auxillary which was a preparation for married life for ladies from about 20 years till they got married. There were church activities but unfortunately, the evidence of the lives of these young ones shows that these groups did not prevent sexual immorality or loose living. I do not say that these programs were not good in themselves; testimonies abound on the blessings and impact they made in the lives of young ones as they grew up. However, nothing can do the work of the Holy Spirit in the life of a man; no activities, no church and no pastor can save a man. They can only be channels in the hands of God, as all men must come to a personal, saving knowledge of the God who owns all life.

Having established that, let me conclude our train of thought on the necessity of the Word of God. Is it not amazing that all through the centuries, everything we see keeps changing: fashions keep adjusting to the demands of society, the world's standards keep moving from one extreme to the other, but all through these, God's standards never change. The standard Abraham was held to was the same Isaiah was held to. The same standard applied to Simon, Peter and Judas Iscariot – disciples of the same man but with two different ends. The same standard is what God is holding up to us too – if we seek Him, we will find Him. That promise was made centuries ago and God is still showing himself strong in the lives of the people who seek Him. **For the eyes of the Lord run to and fro throughout the whole earth, to shew himself strong in the behalf of them whose heart is perfect toward him. Herein thou hast done foolishly: therefore from henceforth thou shalt have wars. - 2 Chronicles 16:9 KJV** What more need be said? Every journey has a starting point and an end point. The journey of life starts from the discovery of what God has to say in His Word.

People, there is a deep well of advice, precepts, commands and teachings preserved in the pages of Scripture and only a careful study, with the help of the author, can unlock the deep wealth hidden in those pages. Abraham heard that author's voice clearly telling him to leave his father's house and go to a place he would be shown. Isaac, his son was also told to remain in a land that had famine. He sowed and reaped in the same year a hundredfold. Jacob, the next in line, had an experience of God and his journey to Laban's place was blessed beyond his wildest expectations.

All Joseph had were the dreams God had given him. They all held on to the Word they had received from God and no wonder that, to this day, we celebrate their lives. For your journey of discovery to make sense, it must start from the Word of God. Read it, study it, memorise it, live it, learn it, do it. One lesson I have also learnt is that God knows our hearts. If you seek God for the wrong reasons, you may never get the best He has for you. A lot of Christians have gotten the order wrong. They think that the blessings they receive from God are directly proportional to the time spent reading the Bible, praying and all. These practices are good and are encouraged. Actually, God will bless you regardless, but what He seeks is a relationship with you based on your love for Him, not on what you can get from Him. One of the reasons there are weak Christians today is that we have been deceived into thinking that as soon as we give our lives to Christ, all problems cease and life becomes heaven. Giving your life to Christ brings heaven to your heart, but on earth where you presently reside, there is a period of hearing, learning and growing that God must take you through for you to be all He has created you to be. Never try to shorten the process, otherwise what you get are Christians who cannot stand the test of time and the pressure of circumstances.

If you have not given your life to Christ, your journey of discovery cannot start. You do not go where you have never been before without a map or a guide. God's Word is both, but its benefits are for those who have made its author their guide. I cannot compel you to accept Christ; I can only tell you that you stand to gain all by accepting Him and to lose all by rejecting Him. The very first verse of the Scripture I ever committed to memory is found in **John 3:16 KJV: For God so Loved the world, that he gave his only begotten Son, that whosoever believeth in him should not perish but have everlasting life.** A short verse but an open invitation to anyone who would come. You have a choice today to choose life or death, blessing or curses. Life is only promised to those who believe in Him, not to those who read about Him or can say a lot about Him. You need a Saviour; you cannot walk this walk or run this race by yourself. If you know you need a Saviour and are ready to receive Christ, just pray this simple prayer: **Lord Jesus, I come to you today. I realise I have been living my life on my terms. I confess I am a sinner and I cannot save myself. Lord Jesus, come into my life and make me a new person. Cleanse me from all my sins and make me a new person. Come into my life and create in me a new heart, ready and willing to obey your commands. I confess you as my Lord and Saviour today. Thank you for coming into my heart. Help me live my life from today as a changed person and make me worthy of heaven. In Jesus' name I pray. Amen.** Now that you have confessed Jesus as your Saviour and Lord, you are ready to start the journey of discovery.

For those already born again, the habit of hearing from God is one you can never outgrow. We can get so caught up in what we are "doing" for God that we forget to take a break and recharge in His presence. Elijah had just done great exploits for God: re-affirmed the worship of Jehovah, dealt a final blow to the worship of Baal by killing all the false prophets and then declared much-welcome rain to King Ahab. All these were done at the command of the Lord, but at the threat of Jezebel, Elijah did not even pause to ask God what he had to do. A man who confronted Ahab's wickedness with God's swift judgment could not wait to hear from God. He ran for his life. That is the summary of a life lived outside the direction of the author of life. The life just keeps running – aimless, directionless and purposeless. What did Elijah get for all his troubles? Eighty days of aimless wandering, only to be sent all the way back to where he had fled and hand over duties to another prophet.

Friends, life is meant to be enjoyed under the watchful guidance of the giver of life itself. We did not make ourselves; the owner and the giver of life is more than capable of giving our lives meaning and direction. We must seek Him out and get the blueprint for our lives. Then we can run our race with conviction, purpose and direction.

One misconception which does need clarifying is from the life of Elijah. I wonder why he had to travel over 80 days just to get to the mountain Horeb, called the Mount of God. Was it that God could only be found there? God is omnipresent – he is everywhere at all times, filling all things in every way. He is not limited by time, space and circumstances, the way men are, or even the devil is. Forget the common notion that Satan also is everywhere. He is a cunning, yet fallen angel who gives the impression that he can play God. He cannot do God because he is not God. We go from place to place, pastor to pastor, prophet to priest, seeking God in the strangest of places. We have been conditioned to think that some people have bought exclusive dialling rights to God's hotline and we must go to or through them to reach God. Until a man finds God for himself, God will only exist as a distant dream or fantasy. So as we take stock of how far God has brought us, His question to us all, as we examine our present standing, is the same question God asked Elijah twice: "What are you doing here, Elijah?" The answer to that question will be determined by the person who has given you the assignment you are on presently. Can you state, without any iota of doubt, that the One who created you inspired your present assignment? Have you heard your father tell you, as His son, what he expects from you? This is a fundamental point to your journey of discovery and until you answer this in the affirmative, you just may end up doing so many things, yet finding no joy in the multitude of activities. Joy does not come from being involved in numerous activities; it comes from finding your niche in God and letting Him take all the glory through you.

HEARING GOD SPEAK

How then does God speak? How do you determine if the directions you have received come from God? We have already established that God speaks in numerous ways, but for the purpose of this book, about four ways will be highlighted and discussed.
These four are: from the Bible, through the Holy Spirit, from the experiences He brings our way or the experiences of other people, and through the body of Christ He has placed us in. We have already discussed one of these ways – experience.

One key lesson here is that we must not limit God to a particular mode or style of speaking. We must not assume that the way He spoke to us yesterday will be the same way He will speak again today. The basis of our relationship with God is the daily discovery of other sides to Him and our discovery of who He is. As we journey on, we discover more about Him and we can recognise His leading and direction in our lives. Other areas will be discussed over the course of this book.

CHAPTER 2

EXPERIENCING GOD – ENVIRONMENT AND EMPOWERMENT

As ye have therefore received Christ Jesus the Lord, so walk ye in him; rooted and built up in him, and stablished in the faith, as ye have been taught, abounding therein with thanksgiving. - Colossians 2:6-7 KJV

The LORD alone led his people without the help of a foreign god. - Deuteronomy 32:12 GNB

And thine ears shall hear a word behind thee, saying, this is the way, walk ye in it - Isaiah 30:21a KJV

I am sure that the joy of any parent is only complete when the child you have given birth to grows over the years. No mother can completely relax if her child remains at the same weight, height and intelligence from birth to the teenage years. There will be a lot of pain, agony and concern as the mother prays that things change for the better. That is the same way with God. When we come to know God, He expects that we also grow in our knowledge of Him. The first verse highlighted above starts with the assumption that you are born again. You are expected to grow in your knowledge of God as you run the race set before you. God expects that I will not remain in one spot for the rest of my life but that as He brings experiences my way, I will grow. Watch the choice of words: *rooted, built up, stablished* and *abounding*. That is the summary of the Christian race and the focus of the rest of this small piece.

When you plant a seed in the ground for the first time, it is assumed that it will grow. Not too many of us who consume processed foods know what has gone into making that food available. We forget that somewhere, someone made a sacrifice to ensure that research was made to find out exactly what was needed to ensure that the end-product of that food was seen. Someone then took time to determine the best conditions under which that seed could thrive and bear fruits. We also forget that someone also took time to ensure that not all the seeds were consumed, but that something was preserved so that the particular food could remain in circulation. We did not consider the fact that someone took time to prepare the ground, put the seed in the soil, watch over it day and night, weed out stuff that could choke the seed and prevent it from bearing fruit, and then prepared a place to preserve the fruit that would be produced. Someone also had task of preparing the fruit for processing, transporting and marketing so it could get to you – the consumer. These are just some of the complexities associated with food. Just imagine then what it took God to make you and bring you to the place where you are now.

When you are born, you too are like a fresh, new seed. God determines the type of ground you are sown in – the country, the environment and most importantly, your immediate family. That is the foundation. God then brings many things your way that are prepared to aid your development – experiences, appointments, disappointments, failures, successes and talents. Unfortunately, you never really take root until you find God. You cannot take to the skies unless you have been properly rooted. That explains why so many people go through life just living and existing, never really settling down to their purpose in life. God formed you as His seed and He alone can help you grow properly. The day you find God, you have been planted by Him where you will find nourishment.

Through all the things He brings your way, you get rooted in Him. You really cannot grow upwards until you have taken root downwards. What does taking root entail? When you know God, you don't rest on your oars. You have got to find out more about His likes, dislikes and the things that make Him tick. We have all had new friends that we wanted to impress. We went out of our way to find out what they liked, and we sometimes pretended we liked the same things they did. You could also look at it like the start of a new love relationship between a man and a woman. A lot of things are shared, time is taken to get to know each other. It is much the same with God, but without the pretence. When we come to know God, it is like the start of a new relationship. The more time you spend with God, the more about Him you get to know. The more you know about Him, the more you do the things that please Him and the more He is pleased with you, the more He blesses you.

It all starts with knowing God. The Bible holds a rich storehouse of knowledge about God that only a careful study of it will reveal. This is another way in which God speaks. As you read its pages, you discover the hand of a God in firm control of the universe, contrary to what the world's system will have you think. As you read it, you will find out why you have been created and put where you are presently. I have seen a scary development among present-day youths. We seem to enjoy "going out" a lot. There are beach parties, excursions to pleasurable places and a lot of games to play. The danger is that we have successfully crowded God out of our lives. We claim to be busy, yet we do not have time to know the things that God wants. How then do we grow? How do we fulfil purpose? How will my life matter when I have not discovered the things that matter to the God who created me and invested so much time, resources and breath in me?

Another danger is starting in God and trying to continue outside of Him. Let me remind you of the words of the passage at the beginning of this chapter: "rooted and built up in Him." That is just fundamental.

You cannot start in Him and try to finish it up on your own. God is not an electrical point with an off and on switch that you can control at will and tell Him where he fits. He is not an impotent God that is subject to man's varied interests and emotions. He calls Himself the Alpha and the Omega for a reason –only the Creator knows how best the created can function and the day the created wants to play the Creator, it is time for the created to be destroyed. A lot of men have become wealthy by the world's standards and now see themselves as "self-made" men, with no input from God. I hear students say that God has got nothing to do with exam success: you read the books, you understood the books and you remembered the books when it mattered most. I think life is much more complicated than that. I had classmates who were smarter than I was but who struggled with remembering tiny details when it mattered most. I had personal experiences of good planning but poor execution. It wasn't always that I did not prepare well, but God had to make me understand that I had to go through Him to become what He wanted me to be. That is one of life's most humbling lessons – that you cannot see beyond your nose and you need help. That is where God comes in.

May we never get to a point where we think that God does not matter. May it never happen that I will get to a point where I feel so self-sufficient that I think I can make it outside of Him. The Bible is replete with stories of men and women who thought they were self-made. Asa, one-time king of Judah, depended so much on God that God made him so powerful.

Unfortunately, power came in and reason went out the window. He was attacked by a foreign king and what was the best he could do? He emptied the treasuries of the temple of the God who helped him, and bribed the king of Egypt, another enemy, to come help him fight. When God warned him of the folly of his actions through a prophet, Asa put the prophet in prison. How did a king who began so well end up so badly? How does a man depend on God to reach the heights of his business or career and then abandon the same God when he gets to the pinnacle? Unfortunately, pretence is an ingrained feature of man, and we have bought the notion that just as we can deceive man, we can also deceive God the same way. You cannot start in God and end up well outside of Him. You cannot depend on God at a time and depend on your abilities the rest of the time. Your life was not made to last that way.

Back to our focal passage for this chapter – Ephesians 2. You need to know why you have been placed where you are and what God has provided for you there. The focal passage makes a reference to having received Christ Jesus as Lord, and continuing to walk in Him. I believe the choice of **IN** and not **WITH** is instructive – you can only mirror the life of someone whose instructions and directives you have completely assimilated. If you claim you have received Christ, it assumes that you have accepted Him as your Lord and Saviour. He owns your life and directs your activities. Daily, you read about Him and His works, you learn about Him and His purposes and priorities. You remain in Him by obeying His instructions and living as He directs. Walking in God connotes an entirety of existence in God, complete submission to His will, and an acceptance of whatever He commands and directs. Does this describe your present situation?

As you remain in God, the flow continues to grow. You are rooted, built up in Him and established, and then overflowing. This is a wonderful picture – you never really remain the same or stay at the same point in your life journey. First, you take root. God places you where He wants you to make maximum impact. He ensures that all that you need to make a change has already been provided. Recall that provision for the position that God has placed you in was settled long before your location was determined. He determined your nationality, your parentage and family background, your skin colour, your peculiar DNA, among several other things. He then placed in you all that you require to be all that He intended. There are no accidents, mistakes or errors.

Wherever you are right now, and whatever you have in your hands at the moment, know that God is not caught by surprise. Everything you know and have now was foreknown by God and He alone can guarantee that you end well. Well, you do have to show up, and be willing to be where, what and who God had ordained you to be. An understanding of your rooting also involves the understanding that even your mistakes are noted and will be used by God to achieve His purpose. With God, nothing is useless. Nothing is without reason. Everything – every situation, every unpleasant experience and everything you call "bad" will be used by God to fulfil His grand plan.

When you have been rooted, the next deliverable in the journey of purpose is to be built up in God. Being built up by God is a lifelong journey. You never outgrow that phase. At no time can you relax, thinking you have arrived or achieved all that you can. In God's school, you never really graduate. At no time do the lessons stop, no matter how "successful" the world calls you. Being built up also takes time, effort and resources. Just as a body builder invests time in daily practice, workouts and exercises, with focus on repetitions and dietary control, the same applies to spiritual building. **1 Timothy 4:8 KJV** talks about bodily exercise and its equivalent in the spiritual: **For bodily exercise profiteth little: but godliness is profitable unto all things, having promise of the life that now is, and of that which is to come**.

It recognises the importance of physical exercise. This does good to the body, as it is a way of keeping fit and staying healthy. All of us have tendencies to grow fat and rotund if we do not have a regimen of regular physical activity that keeps the blood flowing and the body active. It is the same in the spiritual. When you do not have any regimen of spiritual exercise, how do you keep fit? When all you do daily is wake up, rush through the day and spare no thought for God or what He has to say, how do you grow? Spiritual exercise is Godliness – striving to be like God. It is not an overnight experience; it is a lifelong process. You do not arrive there overnight; it is what God does for you throughout your lifetime. No wonder Paul's words here emphasize an ongoing activity, showing that throughout our lives, God is always at work. He is moulding, chiselling, fashioning, breaking, melting, filling and equipping.

Building up can also be a painful experience. When we come to God dirty, full of sin and helpless, do we think that we automatically become perfect all at once? God knows there are things we cannot handle on our own, so He builds up our strength and character through the things He allows us to experience. Character is forged in the dark furnace of trials and tests; character is formed in the silence that accompanies hardships and difficulties. At the end, we appear stronger on the outside, yet we are actually more dependent on God. We appear to be capable, yet what we are is a function of who God is and His work in us.

Ephesians 2:10 KJV says **We are his workmanship**. It does not say we **WERE** (referring to the past) or we **WILL BE** (referring to the future). Right now, we ARE being built up, we ARE being worked on, we ARE being fashioned into His likeness, and we ARE being made to look like Him through the things He brings our way. He has a clear idea of our end purpose; He knows why He has made us who we are and placed us where we are. He never tires; just like the potter, He is always working, so that we can turn out to be exactly what He wants us to be.

ENVIRONMENT AND EMPOWERMENT – How does it work?

In talking about environment and empowerment, there are so many examples from the Bible that we can pick from. A few examples will suffice here:

We see Moses, born at a time of slavery and pressure. He could have been killed in line with the king's command, but God, the potter who knew what lay ahead, stationed God-fearing midwives at the place of his birth. He could have been born anywhere else; God chose the burning cauldron called Egypt. He could have drowned at about a few months old; God stationed Pharaoh's daughter to see him and bring him up as her own. A man born to slaves grew up in the palace of the oppressors. If the story ended like that, we would miss some very important lessons. The environment Moses grew up in prepared him for the assignment God had for him. He grew up in Pharaoh's house and learnt its customs, as he would one day return to see the king and demand freedom for his people. He grew up in Pharaoh's house, but he was taught about the God of the Hebrews by his mother. Every line in the story of Moses in Pharaoh's house speaks of God's amazing wisdom in the location of Moses at this time.

Interestingly, Moses got the timing of the impact wrong. He went out one day, and saw an Egyptian oppressing a fellow Jew. Moses attacked and killed the Egyptian, confident and assured that he was going to clean out the oppressors by His power. Unfortunately, God determines the environment

AND the empowerment. He does not place us where we are without a reason, but rather He ensures that everything that will happen to us will work for our good. When we dare launch out on our own, thinking we've got it locked down, we miss the point, miss the lessons and extend the assignment.

Moses learnt the hard way never to lose sight of what God is doing in regard to time. Moses had to run away from Egypt, and just in case you were wondering how long he ran for, it was 40 years. A man God destined to lead his people out of slavery ended up in the desert, keeping sheep. But here is the light at the end of the tunnel – every experience of Moses was used by God to bring His own purpose to pass. Moses learnt how to take care of sheep – lead them out, find pasture for them and nurture them daily. It was a preparation for the human version of keeping sheep. There would be pressure, there would be angry moments, there would be times when the people rebelled and rejected his leadership. Taking care of sheep for 40 years prepared him for leading God's people for another 40 years.

On a very sombre note, is it not a bit frightening that Moses still did not enter the Promised Land? If he could bear the people's excesses for a while, why would he allow anger to destroy what he had put together? At this time, I think it is proper for you the reader to pause here and consider – if God could stop Moses, a man with whom He spoke face to face, a man He had empowered and placed in a particular place and at a particular time to fulfil a particular purpose, how do we imagine that we could escape if we do what Moses did?

Another good example is Apostle Paul. He explodes with violence into the scenes of the early church, persecuting those who were Christians. He was an active participant in the stoning to death of Stephen, and thereafter picked up letters to go to Damascus and arrest all those who belonged to the Way of Christ. However, the potter had other plans. He was waiting for Saul on the way, and one encounter with Jesus changed Saul's life. Later on in his letters, he gave a vivid description of God's placement and empowerment in his life: **For we are the circumcision, which worship God in the spirit, and rejoice in Christ Jesus, and have no confidence in the flesh. Though I might also have confidence in the flesh. If any other man thinketh that he hath whereof he might trust in the flesh, I more: Circumcised the eighth day, of the stock of Israel, of the tribe of Benjamin, an Hebrew of the Hebrews; as touching the law, a Pharisee; Concerning zeal, persecuting the church; touching the righteousness which is in the law, blameless. – Philippians 3:3-6 KJV**

The above passage is a classic example of God at work. Everything in Paul's life pointed to what God had ahead for him. All the training, exposure and fearlessness were leading up to the mission Paul had – preaching without fear, speaking with authority and having the clout to stand before the great men of his day.

Can we consider the life of Joseph? Here was a man of lofty dreams, a man with a clear idea of the greatness that lay ahead. You would expect his life to follow a course of great events and mighty acts, right? Wrong! His brothers conspired to kill him; when that plan did not work, they kept him in a pit and then sold him as a prisoner to Egypt. In Egypt, he worked as a servant in Potiphar's house. Pause here and think – how did a man with such lofty dreams sink to such depths of despair and desolation? How did a dream of greatness descend to the depths of grinding despair?

We are indeed limited in scope, experience, impact and reason. We always assume that God will take us through familiar routes that will look like where He is taking us to. We put God in a box, thinking He has to be logical, reasonable and practical in the way He thinks. When this route does not look like what we think it will, we begin to ask questions, or we think we have gone wrong somewhere. We spend so much time looking inwards and castigating ourselves that we do not see what God is doing around us. Joseph left the pit for Potiphar's house, then from Potiphar's house, rather than go higher, he then went down to prison. Trust me, it takes a clear knowledge of God's working, power and grace to accept His working in our lives. But you know what? One great lesson from the life of Joseph, with great impact on the issue under consideration, is the phrase that runs through the story of Joseph – **"And the Lord was with him."** That is the most important part of the story.

You will amount to nothing if you are empty of the presence and power of God. From the pit to Potiphar's house to the prison, and then to the palace as Prime Minister, God's presence and power was the defining factor in Joseph's life. It does not matter how deep you go, or how high you go, the fulfilment of your destiny is tied to the understanding of your environment and empowerment. Wherever you are right NOW, you have been placed there by God for a purpose; there are lessons to learn where you are right now. There are character traits God has to build in you where you are right now. There are virtues that you must imbibe and personalise in order to make them a blessing where you are going. Towards the end of his life, Joseph looked back and realised that indeed, God was at work all around him, long before he even realised the scope of his purpose and the extent of the influence God was working in him to accomplish.

It is fitting to make Jesus our final example. His story is simple, yet earth-moving. Here we find the King of Kings and the Creator of the ends of the earth stooping so low as to be born in a manger. It was so shocking that the whole world did not recognise God at work. Herod was thinking of a potential coup and an appropriate response to the news of another king while he was still reigning. The wise men from the east came looking for the right King but in the wrong palace. The inn-keepers were probably more concerned about making money, as all the rooms were fully booked. Even the manger became a resting place for interested parties. The world was sitting idly away, while God was at work changing the destiny of anyone who would believe in and accept the birth of the One who would save the world from sin. Ordinary shepherds received the good news before princes and kings who were not ready. A virgin maiden and an upright man were being prepared by God to be the vessels for His miracle.

There is something very peculiar about the environment and empowerment of Jesus at His birth. These wise men came bearing gifts for a baby they had not seen, but had only seen his star. All that Jesus would come to mean, and all He would do on earth was spoken of prophetically by the gifts these wise men gave. One big lesson – God does not make mistakes with wherever He has placed me. If He is the determinant of where I am, He will ensure that I get everything my location requires in order to be effective and purposeful. The whole idea of Colossians 2:6-7 is to emphasise what is important in your life – you do not go far in life without God and you cannot make it in life outside of God. It does not matter what the world thinks is important; all that matters is what God says, and He has disclosed His will by his Word.

MOVING FORWARD

If I have accepted Jesus as Lord and Saviour, then I am on the right path to discover more of God and grow in God. As I take root below and bear fruit above, the world just has to notice the difference in me. As **Matthew 5:16 KJV** says: **Let your light so shine before men, that they may see your good works, and glorify your Father which is in heaven.** Let me quickly point this out – your light is not about you; it is about Jesus who is the Light of the world. Your light shining means Jesus shining out of you, the world noticing a difference and seeking out that light in you. At all times, it must be clear that you are not promoting yourself or your own interests; you are seeking to bring glory to God through your life.

WHY AM I WHERE I AM NOW?

As we have established, God does not make mistakes. Everything that has gone into your rooting, establishment, building up and overflowing will all work towards the achievement of our God-ordained purpose. Unfortunately, we can go through life rudderless and seemingly without direction. We fold our arms and watch life happens, holding on to the incorrect notion that whatever God has ordained will work out fine without any input whatsoever from us. There is nothing we can do to change God's purpose for our lives, but you can be sure that you have to take time to discover exactly what God wants for you and take time to pursue exactly that. That is the fundamental principle of **Philippians 2:12-13 KJV**; verses that talk about God's role and man's responsibility:

Wherefore, my beloved, as ye have always obeyed, not as in my presence only, but now much more in my absence, work out your own salvation with fear and trembling. For it is God which worketh in you both to will and to do of his good pleasure.

Man has a duty to discover his placing, his environment, his opportunities, his strengths and his weaknesses. God will always make the appropriate resources available for the man who is where he is rightly placed. One of the gravest dangers of this generation is the contemporary messages of prosperity and progress without accountability or responsibility. We tell others that God is a God who wants His children to be rich and wealthy. We don't talk about the right definition and source of wealth or the right channels to wealth. We now have a possession-conscious generation, people with an entitlement mentality. We do not walk right or live right or talk right, yet we want to live plentiful lives and have all that we want. God does not give us all we ask for; He expects us to ask in faith for all that we need and He wants us to have. When we are rightly located, when we are where He has placed us at the time He wants us to make an impact, then the resources that are appropriate for the place we are will be provided.

The importance of getting your environment right cannot be overemphasised. Imagine for a moment that John the Baptist had stayed in the city to preach; it is possible that he may not have made the kind of impact he did during his very short public ministry. He was in the desert, yet men were trooping there to listen to him. He ate locusts and wild honey, yet he spoke with a clarity and preciseness that only a man working and walking where God put him could inspire. Herod feared him, the Pharisees and teachers of the law, including the tax collectors were not spared the truth. He spoke the truth to power, he dared to express all that God put in him. Can that be said about you?

There is a craze travelling out of Africa at the moment. Things are getting more and more difficult by the day. Years of systematic pillaging, lawlessness and looting has finally caught go with us. While nations were busy putting aside seed for further sowing, we were busy eating the whole harvest. Now, there is no seed left to sow and of course, limited food to go around. But you know what? In the midst of this mess, God's Word sounds loud and clear – I am not bound by the economy or the state of finances. For everyone else, it was a land of famine, to Isaac, it was a time to be where God wanted him to be. People will advise you to be wise and be rightly located, using indices that the world has tested and found true. The world will tell you to be smart by engaging in courses that are contemporary for the age we are in. Whilst there is nothing wrong with that, that should not be our greatest pursuit. A Harvard degree may get you the best the world has to offer, but God can disgrace the degree just to prove a point. You may be rightly located by the standards of the world and yet have nothing flowing your way because you are NOT located where God's provision can reach you.

This is a fundamental truth: God's provision and sustenance is tied to our being rightly located on His terms. Our environment will divinely provide what we require to fulfil our purpose. When God hands out His provision for an assignment that He needs done in Nigeria, and you have relocated to Canada, how will the provision in Nigeria reach you? Isaac learnt that lesson rightly – if God is the one determining your environment, you are assured of his empowerment. Isaac sowed in a land where there was famine and yet reaped a hundredfold of what he sowed. It does not matter what the economy is saying; it does not matter what the state of your finances are; it does not matter how many closed doors you see; what is important is the clarity of your location and empowerment. If you are where you are expected to be, you will get what you are entitled to.

Let us be clear about something – being where God places you does not make you immune from trials and tribulations. The fact that you are located rightly does not mean that everything around you will always start out right and end right. I am not advocating against relocation. Move if you must, but like Lot, don't let temporary discomfort or the deceitful look of the moment deceive you into moving out of God's perfect place for you.

CHAPTER 3

WHO AM I TO GO WITH?

In light of what we have examined earlier, you will agree with me that purpose and impact are intricately tied to encouragers. God will always give a person an assignment, and then assign helpers along the way to assist in the fulfilment of the purpose. Of course, what other authority exists on the subject matter, apart from God Himself? Let us discover together the purpose of God on the matter of encouragement and purpose.

Then the Lord God formed the man from the dust of the ground. He breathed the breath of life into the man's nostrils, and the man became a living person. Then the Lord God planted a garden in Eden in the east, and there he placed the man he had made.

The Lord God made all sorts of trees grow up from the ground – trees that were beautiful and that produced delicious fruit. In the middle of the garden he placed the tree of life and the tree of

the knowledge of good and evil. A river flowed from the land of Eden, watering the garden and then dividing into four branches. The first branch, called the Pishon, flowed around the entire land of Havilah, where gold is found. The gold of that land is exceptionally pure; aromatic resin and onyx stone are also found there. The second branch, called the Gihon, flowed around the entire land of Cush. The third branch, called the Tigris, flowed east of the land of Asshur. The fourth branch is called the Euphrates.

The Lord God placed the man in the Garden of Eden to tend and watch over it. But the Lord God warned him, "You may freely eat the fruit of every tree in the garden – except the tree of the knowledge of good and evil. If you eat its fruit, you are sure to die." Then the Lord God said, "It is not good for the man to be alone. I will make a helper who is just right for him."

So the Lord God formed from the ground all the wild animals and all the birds of the sky. He brought them to the man to see what he would call them, and the man chose a name for each one. He gave names to all the livestock, all the birds of the sky, and all the wild animals. But still there was no helper just right for him.

So the Lord God caused the man to fall into a deep sleep. While the man slept, the Lord God took out one of the man's ribs and closed up the opening. Then the Lord God made a woman from

the rib, and he brought her to the man. "At last!" the man exclaimed. "This one is bone from my bone, and flesh from my flesh! She will be called 'woman,' because she was taken from 'man.'" This explains why a man leaves his father and mother and is joined to his wife, and the two are united into one. - Genesis 2:7-24 NLT

From the account above, quite a number of lessons pop out, highlighting the importance of getting it right from the beginning. First of all, God made man and gave him His own breath, then gave him work to do and an environment within which he was to work. Man was given all the tools required to make an impact where he was placed. There was a world to nurture, a garden to tend and creation to improve. First lesson: you cannot tamper with the divine order. You have got to know your appropriate location and assignment before you can properly situate your company. Too many times, we allow friends to determine what we want to do in life. We want to be accepted by friends and society; we do not want to upset the regular mill of society. Unfortunately, a life lived for the pleasure and joy of other people's opinions will always lack direction and impact.

Note also that in the midst of the assignment was the no-go area. God did not wait for man to receive his companion before He gave him the rules of engagement. The man had received instructions on what he was to do, the place and scope of his assignment, and the limitations of the assignment. That is another lesson – with God, there are no vague, universally applicable instructions when it comes to purpose. The reason why the Bible is so instructive is because it speaks to God's plan for all mankind. It encourages us to seek out God's specific plan for our lives. What God does is to make a PRO VISION – that is, what we require **for** (pro) the specific **vision** that he has given us. Yes, there really are general instructions for life in the Word of God, but I have learnt that God will give definite instructions from His Word to specific individuals who seek to know God in their daily walk with Him. What works for one person is not guaranteed to work for another person, because both of them are different in design, assignment, placement, gifting and companionship.

This can be aptly seen in the story of Abraham and Lot:

The Lord had said to Abram, "Leave your native country, your relatives, and your father's family, and go to the land that I will show you. So Abram departed as the Lord had instructed, and Lot went with him. Abram was seventy-five years old when he left Haran. - Genesis 12:1-4 NLT

We have looked at the account of the beginning of creation, yet we see the lessons from that account brought to the fore in the passage above. God came to Abraham and asked him to leave the familiar surroundings of family, as He had great purposes for him that his present location could not comprehend or contain. God could bless him in Haran if that was his purpose, but God wanted to bring him to a place that would be fit and proper for what God wanted to do. And so, Abraham took off as he had been commanded, and Lot went with him.

I have heard it argued that there was nothing wrong in Lot going with Abraham. The young guy must have seen that God was with his uncle and wanted to associate with him. Well, I believe that this was the first recorded time that God spoke to Abraham. Terah, Abraham's father could have received an instruction to go to Canaan, because at a point in time, he took his entire family on a journey in that direction. However, he got to Haran and settled and eventually died there. I do not want to assume that God told Terah to move, and I wouldn't know why he settled somewhere in the middle of the journey. The Bible makes no reference to any incidence of such. One thing is however clear – purpose is personal. Instructions are general and are universally applicable, but if your life must matter beyond the general and the ordinary; you cannot settle for non-specifics. You really have to dig deep and find out where God would have you be, what He would have you do, and who you are to go with.

Back to Abraham and Lot. Why did Lot go with Abraham or why did Abraham agree to go with Lot? Abraham received the instruction to leave his father's house; why did he take along relics of his father's house? The best of intentions do not make purpose any clearer. Lot may have had the best of intentions, but when you consider his end, you may wonder if he truly was best served to have gone with Abraham on that journey. Eventually, a separation had to occur, due to frequent quarrels between the herdsmen of both Abraham and Lot. A decision had to be made. This was the moment when personal vision spoke so clearly. Lot was asked to choose which direction he wanted to go, and like the clueless person he was, he choose a location based purely on physical, ephemeral conditions. The layout of the land before him determined the layout of his life. Though it appeared to be a good decision initially, the end showed just how foolish his decision was.

Before we criticise Lot, let us examine our lives closely. Can we honestly say that God ordained our present pursuits? Can we truly say that we are where God intends for us to be? Friends and peers hold a large part of our hearts and we want to please them. That's good, as long as they are pushing you to the discovery and fulfillment of God's purpose for your life. Where they are not, you owe it to yourself to discover, pursue and fulfil God's plan for your life.

This is what God does – He takes an individual on a journey of discovery. The individual walks with God and God shows him great and wonderful things. Sometime in the future, God will bring another person the way of that first individual, who will further strengthen the work that God has already begun. In effect, God can prepare people of purpose in different climes and regions, and sometime in the future, bring them all together for the fulfilment of His own purpose. The individual purpose is not lost; it is simply there to make greater impact in the scope of the corporate assignment. Like it has been said, if you do not have a clear idea of your own vision, how can you ever understand your role in another person's life?

Therefore, in the course of the pursuit of God's purpose for my life, I will require input, advice or help from another person of purpose. Lot was content following his uncle about, yet in the end, it was obvious that he had no direction, and no clear idea of his purpose. He was making eternal decisions on ephemeral, empirical evidence. To him, the land of Sodom and Gomorrah looked like the garden of the Lord. He went into the land full of herds, servants and property; he left with only his two daughters. To further accentuate how far he had fallen, his daughters applied what they had learnt from living in Sodom and had children by their father. That decision also had eternal consequences, as both children arising from this ungodly alliance of father and daughters birthed the Moabites and the Ammonites, who would later become arch enemies of Israel. O, what grave consequences arise from a life without purpose and direction. What grave consequences await a life without input from God, a life lived without accountability, responsibility and eternity in view.

This also is established from the story of Abraham and Lot. Friends, helpers, companions and vision helpers were not brought your way to replace your vision. Too often, we lose focus simply because we cannot define the limits and scope of engagement for someone who was brought into our lives. Trust me, you were not created to be the answer to ALL of life's problems. You were created to be the solution to a particular issue at a particular time, and all that God will send to you will work towards that purpose. Even if God would have you suspend the pursuit of one assignment for the temporary pursuit of another assignment, it will never negate the purpose of God for your life or go against what He has already established in His Word.

You owe it to God and the generation God has determined for you to bless to ensure that you identify the place and limits of all persons He brings your way. Some come into your life for a reason, some come for a season while others come to help with a required decision. You must know which person fits into which category. Some people come to provide clarity to the vision God gives you and then inexplicably, they walk away. Some people are sent to hold your hand, to help you through a particular patch. Others come in and help you in a decision-making process. Whatever the reason, never forget – purpose is personal. People will come into your life at different times and seasons, but when you know what and where God is leading, you will not be moved by a desire to impress anyone or to hold tightly to anyone. When the purpose of an individual in your life ends, God will orchestrate events that will lead to the person leaving. Don't force issues, don't hold on too tightly. If God is involved, nothing will be too precious to let go of, so you can hold on to that which is God's perfect will.

Back to the first family of Genesis 2. Man was created long after all that he needed to thrive and survive was already in place. God did not think of what man would need and then struggle to provide for him; provisions were already in place when man was placed and commissioned on assignment. Man got to work, naming creatures, cultivating the land and taking care of his environment. Then, God realised man was alone. I do not know how we found this independence that leads us to believe that we are masters of our own destinies and do not need God. We now determine for ourselves what course to pursue, who to marry, where to settle, what to do and how we will get it done. It is almost as if God's opinions do not count anymore. That is the dangerous trend we are pursuing these days, in the name of awareness and independence.

We can never outgrow our need for God and His help, if we are to fulfil purpose and make an impact. God worked through the entire process of placing man where He wanted him, then sorted out his material and human resources. God is still in the business of sorting out these delicate matters and we will only be blessed when we work with God in these matters. Everyone God intends that will help you in the discovery and fulfilment of purpose will be sorted out by Him in His own time, not yours. He will bring the people on his own terms, not yours. Remember, the assignment is His in the first place, you are just privileged to be counted worthy of being a vessel He can use.

Does the Bible have other lessons on the same subject matter? Check out the story of Samson. A classic example of inconsistencies. When Samson was in trouble, he would sometimes call on God for help but at other times, he would simply depend on brute strength. Unfortunately, you cannot go through living like that. Purpose is not something to be pursued on a whim. You don't choose how and when you pursue your purpose. You just have to do it on God's own terms. However, our focus is on Samson. How did a man chosen by God go so wrong? His parents warned him about his association with a Philistine woman but his mind was made up. Well, the Bible records that **his father and mother didn't realise the Lord was at work in this, creating an opportunity to work against the Philistines, who ruled over Israel at that time. - Judges 14:4 NLT**

I will not question God's purpose in this, but there is no doubt that God does not work against the exercise of a man's free will. Samson had already cast his eyes over the Philistine woman and would not listen. But God still worked out His purpose, even in the midst of all the stubbornness and headiness of Samson. Then came Delilah. If God was at work in the case of Samson's Philistine wife, how do you explain this evil woman? The entire story reveals the grave consequences of aligning with the wrong persons, no matter how noble their intentions are.

However, there will also be friends who believe in your vision and offer themselves willingly to assist. You just must know who is expected to work with you. Gideon is a classic example. Here is a man with no war pedigree, no prior experience in warfare, yet

God sent him to go deliver Israel from the Midianites. Therein lay the dilemma – how does a man like Gideon prepare for war? Of course, like every typical person. He went to the farthest regions of the land, asking that all able-bodied men report to camp. I'm sure that when he saw the thirty-two thousand people who reported to camp, he was glad. Then came the shocker – not all who reported to camp were destined for the particular purpose God was calling Gideon to. The process of whittling down began. The God who calls and equips decided that only 300 people were up for the task at hand. To make matters even worse, God asked the men to give up their weapons and take up pitchers and trumpets.

I cannot definitively determine what went through the mind of Gideon as God was decimating his support. Who would take a knife to a gunfight? When a man comes against you with guns, wouldn't you at least try and match him, if not outdo him? Meet the God who shames effort just to prove that He is all that we need. Meet the God who determines who and what we need in the pursuit of His own purpose for our lives. After all, it is His purpose, His will, His plan that we are pursuing. Why then do we think we know what and who is best for that assignment?

The need to also understand the place of the companions that God will bring your way, in the course of pursuing your purpose, is also seen in the life of David and Jonathan. How do you explain the friendship between the heir apparent to the throne and a rival young lad, whose only claim to the throne was an anointing witnessed only by the immediate family members of the young lad? Jonathan confessed that he knew David would be king after his father, yet he clung in friendship to David, even in the face of his father's attempted murder of him because of his "friendship with the enemy".

You would expect this friendship to continue forever. However, as we have established, you must know the reason or the season for every resource that God brings your way. In God's purpose for David, maybe Jonathan had no input and had to depart the scene. He died a painful death, due to no apparent fault of his. This holds a deep lesson for me: no friendship, no matter how deep or precious, can replace the pursuit of purpose. You can hold on for as long as you want, you may desire the friendship and companionship of any man. However, in the words of Myles Munroe in his book *The Principles and Power of Vision*- "**people who change the world have declared independence from other people's expectations.**" Do you have a clear idea of what you are? Do you know who you belong to? Have you settled the issue of your identity and location, so that you are set free from the burden of pleasing people, and you can pursue God's purpose and direction for your life? These questions are fundamental to your destiny and the answers to them may well determine the direction your life will take going forward.

Can we talk again about Joseph and his experiences in Egypt? Every time I read his story, I learn something new. Here was a young lad who was given birth to after years of waiting. His mother, though loved by the father, could not conceive for a while. After his birth, the father could not help but favour Joseph over his older brothers, and of course, as is typical of large, polygamous families, sibling rivalry slowly became deadly. In the process, Joseph learnt to dream and to discuss the dreams with all who cared to listen, even his father. Those dreams were tied to his purpose in life, but he had no idea how things would pan out. The question I would have asked under this heading is: couldn't the dreams be fulfilled in his father's house? Why did he have to go through all he went through, just because he had a destiny to fulfil? The answer that becomes apparent to me is that he could not continue in the same vein with his brothers and still fulfill his purpose. These were his blood brothers, yet they had no part to play in the preparation for the season of manifestation. All they had to do was point him in the right direction, which was Egypt. After that, it was all God pulling the strings and orchestrating events to work out what He had planned.

I cannot overemphasise this: you were not sent to everybody; you are not the answer to all of life's problems; you don't have all the answers to all of life's questions. God alone fits the bill. All I can do is discover and pursue what God intends. The word provision was mentioned earlier and it bears mentioning again – provision is tied to vision, not to wants. If what I am asking God for is not appropriate for the assignment He has given me, He is not under obligation to give it to me. I can keep banging my head against the wall or I can just accept that I am not the answer to life for everyone. I must accept my limitations and rest on God's limitless resources.

Joseph's depth was tested by his experiences away from home. He was pampered by his father, but matured by his experiences. When he was in prison, he felt unjustly treated and pleaded with the cupbearer of the king to remember him. And yet, three days later, when the cupbearer was released, he completely forgot Joseph. If you dare to depend on human connections and what people can do for you, you are set up to fail woefully. If all you can do is call on man for help, then you have not met the God who disappoints the devices of men just to prove a point. If you cannot live outside the scope of men's approval or ratings, then you have a long way to go.

Moses also comes to mind here. I think this man was really complex. He started with a strong desire to deliver his people from bondage but he went about it the wrong way. He then had to learn meekness and patience by leading sheep. When the call eventually came to lead the Israelites to the Promised Land, he could not summon the courage to go. God had to practically guarantee that Moses would have the support of someone with him on the journey to the land of promise. Check out the entire life of Moses after his commission – there was Aaron, there was Jethro, there was Hur and there was Joshua. At different times and as the occasion demanded, God always raised people to support His people of vision.

When God commissions an assignment, He knows that the assignment is bigger than one man. No one is so endowed that s/he has everything he needs to fulfil God's purpose for his life. We all need assistance; and that could be from someone else, a group of persons or a community. Whatever it is, God will always bring your way other people of vision that will also help in the fulfilment of your own vision. Because all the visions are from God, they are all interlinked, and the fulfilment of one God-ordained vision means the fulfilment of other linked God-ordained visions.

Can we also talk about Jesus and his disciples? These were men chosen after a series of nights of prayers. The assignment had been determined, the environment had been sorted and the endowment required to be effective had been provided. It was time to choose those who would stay with Him, learn under Him and become His disciples. Isn't it humbling that a man like Judas Iscariot was there? Of course, there were also the three main parties – Peter, James and John.

You can spend the whole day learning and reading about God and yet God will not know you as His own. You can spend the whole week in church, and yet the owner of the church will not identify you as His own. These twelve disciples were not the best that God could have chosen by human standards, but for the sake of purpose, these men had to be called out. You may have been chosen to lead a group or to pastor a congregation, based on your skills and experiences. However, please note that in pursuing this assignment, the God factor is key. Whatever God ordains, He sustains. Whatever He inspires, he will make proper provision for the inspiration to find expression and fulfilment.

Just in case it did not stick the first time, let me repeat this again for emphasis: there is a reason and a season for everyone and everything God brings your way in your pursuit of purpose. If you do not understand these seasons, you will hold on to people and situations long after their season or reason has passed. If you are not sensitive to how God leads you, you will probably not appreciate the worth of the relationships God brings your way.

CHAPTER 4

WHAT AM I HERE FOR, AT THIS VERY POINT IN TIME?

Here we stand, at the point of decision. With all you have read here, and the many more words you will hear across the various media and channels available, what is your decision? I believe it has been established that you just don't exist; you are a fundamental part of God's plan, formulated long before you were born, and will continue long after you are either raptured or dead physically. God's promise of eternal life proves without a doubt that there is no end to His eternal purpose. He began his work long before the world we know it began, and He will continue it long after the world as we know it now, ceases to exist.

You owe it to God to discover your place in His eternal plan. You cannot wake up every morning without a clear idea of what you are convinced God wants you to be doing. You do not need to take giant steps; what you need are daily small steps, taking you gradually to the place God intends for you. You may not get it right every time; in fact, most days, you may feel that you have not moved any further than where you were a few years ago, but as we have already established, your emotions and feelings are not the best assurance when it comes to the certainty of your eternal purpose. God's opinion and assurance is the only thing you need as you walk the walk, run the race and fight the good fight of faith.

I want to share with you a few of the lessons God has taught me over the few years of walking with Him. I confess here again, just as I did at the beginning of this book, that I am not the authority on what God says about himself and his plans; HE is. What He has to say on any matter is more important than what my intellectual capacity can comprehend or postulate. The wealth and treasures available in His Word cannot be fully mined by any individual, no matter how much of God s/he knows, or how much of Himself God chooses to reveal. I have learnt that I can never outgrow my need for God, and I can never become independent of His grace and the help of the Holy Spirit.

There are five lessons shared below, extracted from various Bible passages that discuss God's role in the eternal plan, my role in the complex arrangement, and how I can be relevant and impactful in my lifetime on earth. In the course of discussing these lessons, these roles will be highlighted. Come with me on this journey of discovery:

LESSON ONE

His Presence and His Presents

The company of the prophets said to Elisha, "Look, the place where we meet with you is too small for us. Let us go to the Jordan, where each of us can get a pole; and let us build a place there for us to meet." And he said, "Go." Then one of them said, "Won't you please come with your servants?" "I will," Elisha replied. And he went with them. They went to the Jordan and began to cut down trees. As one of them was cutting down a tree, the iron axe head fell into the water. "Oh no, my Lord!" he cried out. "It was borrowed!" The man of God asked, "Where did it fall?" When he showed him the place, Elisha cut a stick and threw it there, and made the iron float. "Lift it out," he said. Then the man reached out his hand and took it. - 2 Kings 6:1-7 NIV

Quick lessons:

1. When you are working for God, there is a guarantee that you will grow. The growth will not always be what you expect, but when you open your heart and life to God, He makes you into the person that He intends, so that you can bring Him glory through the way you live your life. For these sons of prophets, the growth here was physical, mental and spiritual.

2. God will bless your going out and your coming in, not your sitting down and grumbling about the economy. Do something about where you are presently. Write that book, take that course, do that thing you have been putting off for years. God's 100% multiplied by your own 0% will amount to nothing. The sons of the prophets recognised a need, and took steps to address it.

3. Be sure of who you are going with. Some of life's greatest projects and assignments have been destroyed simply by the wrong association. The fact that God has inspired your present pursuit does not mean that the whole world must join hands with you in the pursuit of that purpose. Choose your destiny helpers carefully; your eternal success may depend on it. The sons of the prophets would not step out without Elisha; Moses would not go forward without God's sure presence, Oluwaseun here will not do anything without God's sure presence. What of you?

4. The presence of God does not insure you from trouble; His glory is magnified through it. If you are looking for a trouble-free life, you may need to vacate the earth. Everywhere you turn, there are issues. Yet, in all of these, God says He has overcome, so I need not fear. Looking at God's pedigree, I think I would rather trust in God than trust what my environment says. Elisha was there, yet the axe head still fell. God is present, yet you may not feel His presence.

You look for him through the tears, and it appears God is sitting on his hands. Lazarus was dying, yet his friend Jesus was strolling about, seemingly unconcerned. Debts are rising, things are hard, and God seems so far away. Any of the above sounds familiar?

5. The miracle you need is just a prayer, a cry, a word in the right direction. We talk about our problems to people who mostly don't care or to people with their own baggage, or people who are even happy that you have those problems. God is the only one who can help you, because He has been found to be faithful. Everything has its own season, even your pains and your discomfort. The sons of prophets cried to Elisha, Elisha looked to God and God did the heavy lifting. All they needed was to speak out.

6. God does not need the usual, the obvious and the known to prove His power. How does a stick make an iron head float? How does a fiery furnace become an air-conditioned room? How does a den of lions become a room for the night? I really cannot say, but what I know is this: long before science tried to make sense of this world, God had been at work. He does as He pleases, with whatever He pleases and with whomever He pleases. He takes a little boy's lunch and feeds thousands with it, He turns a fish into an Automated Teller Machine (ATM) to pay temple tax, He covenants with an ordinary man, and blesses him so much that generations after him are still tapping

into those same blessings. Meet the God who parted the Red Sea simply because His people needed to leave bondage. Meet the God who sends down fire to burn up the entire altar of stones, the sacrifice on it and the water from 12 large jars of water that had been poured on everything. Pray, tell me, how do you light a fire on something that has been soaked in water? Now, that is God. He speaks through whomever and whatever is available and surrendered to Him.

Have you met this God? Do you know Him? Better still, does He know you? God does not prove Himself by popular opinion, so if you mistake the applause of men for the favour of God, you will have missed one of life's most important experiences – the presence of God. You really need His presence if His presents are to make sense. What he gives you as presents are not as important as his presence; we seem more willing to milk God for what He can give us than who He can be in our lives. Both are important, but one is an integral part of our lives, ensuring that the other makes sense.

LESSON TWO

Check Your Standards

And he shewed me Joshua the high priest standing before the angel of the Lord, and Satan standing at his right hand to resist him. And the Lord said

unto Satan, The Lord rebuke thee, O Satan; even the Lord that hath chosen Jerusalem rebuke thee: is not this a brand plucked out of the fire? Now Joshua was clothed with filthy garments, and stood before the angel. And he answered and spake unto those that stood before him, saying, Take away the filthy garments from him. And unto him he said, Behold, I have caused thine iniquity to pass from thee, and I will clothe thee with change of raiment. And I said, Let them set a fair mitre upon his head. So they set a fair mitre upon his head, and clothed him with garments. And the angel of the Lord stood by. And the angel of the Lord protested unto Joshua, saying, Thus saith the Lord of hosts; If thou wilt walk in my ways, and if thou wilt keep my charge, then thou shalt also judge my house, and shalt also keep my courts, and I will give thee places to walk among these that stand by. - Zechariah 3:1-7 KJV

Quick Lessons:

1. Satan does not always need a legal ground to stand before God and seek to harm us. Our service, dedication and absolute devotion to God does not guarantee us safety from Satan's roving eye.

2. God alone is the one who can rebuke the devil and cause his work to cease in our lives. He is the one who knows us so well that He can address the root cause of our problems, which is the power of sin. Working in God's house or

working for God is not in itself sufficient; you must first settle the issue of your foundations.

3. You can successfully deceive many people, but God cannot be deceived. He knows our strengths and weaknesses, and the sincerity of our hearts. Joshua was standing before the angel of the Lord "serving", yet his garments were filthy. Are you properly attired? Are you dressed ready for service as determined by God? There are several of us today doing the same thing in God's house – behaving insincerely, untruthfully and hypocritically, yet "busy" at work in God's house and minding God's business. We have mastered the art of deception, and give the impression that we are working for God. It is not enough to claim to know God; you had better be sure that God knows you.

Do you even know that you are at war? Are you content with coasting through life, neither hot nor cold, but just content to get by on the minimum of standards? Before the devil eats you up for breakfast, you had better make amends.

Let us also consider this: what made the priestly office special? It appears that both the outer garments and the conduct of the office were important. Can we be wrongly dressed for service and still offer quality service to God? We have suddenly begun to defend ourselves, claiming that it is the heart that is important, not how we dress. How did we get to this point? Where is the place of the armour of God? Where is the place of being adorned with good works, the kind befitting those who confess the Lord's name? Do we focus so much on the inside that we think the outside does not matter at all? Was it not the behavior of the Antioch believers that made people around them call them "Christians"? When people look at you or move around you, do you need to shout from the rooftops that you are a child of God, or does your light shine so strongly that people cannot ignore it?

4. Before Joshua could be properly restored, there had to be a cleansing, a purification, and a change of clothes. You cannot come to God on your own terms, negotiating a deal with God or surrendering just a part of your life to Him for renewal. It has to be everything. God must take the whole life or you will be of no use to Him. A surrendered life is the most useful tool in God's hands, not necessarily the most skilled or the most educated.

5. The blessings are there for the taking, by all who will surrender to God and obey Him absolutely. We claim God's promises while boldly living in sin; we seek to bribe God by paying fat tithes out of ill-gotten wealth; we have turned God's gifts primarily into a money-making venture instead of first seeking to glorify Him with the gifts.

6. God's plans are always steeped in eternity. Nowhere do records state that God entered into a covenant with man and did not make

a reference to the past, present and future. God settled a course of life for me; He brought me forth to fulfill that purpose, so that His eternal plans could be brought alive in the hearts of men. I cannot thrive without that consciousness; if I am only conscious of the earthly and temporal, I have not understood fully what God is all about. Don't just claim promises blindly; fulfill the conditions and you will see God bringing the fulfillment of the promises your way.

LESSON THREE

Living the Life

Praise ye the Lord. Blessed is the man that feareth the Lord, that delighteth greatly in his commandments. His seed shall be mighty upon earth: the generation of the upright shall be blessed. Wealth and riches shall be in his house: and his righteousness endureth forever. Unto the upright there ariseth light in the darkness: he is gracious, and full of compassion, and righteous. A good man sheweth favour, and lendeth: he will guide his affairs with discretion. Surely he shall not be moved forever: the righteous shall be in everlasting remembrance. He shall not be afraid of evil tidings: his heart is fixed, trusting in the Lord. His heart is established, he shall not be afraid, until he see his desire upon his enemies. He hath dispersed, he hath given to the poor; his

righteousness endureth for ever; his horn shall be exalted with honour. The wicked shall see it, and be grieved; he shall gnash with his teeth, and melt away: the desire of the wicked shall perish. - Psalms 112:1-10 KJV

Quick Lessons:

You cannot separate the fear of God from the diligent study and obedience of His Word. How would you even fear someone you do not know, or whose likes and dislikes you do not know?

Fear of God has a generational impact. My actions today are seeds that generations after me will reap. I had better watch what I sow now; my children may have to live with the eternal consequences of my actions today.

When you have sown the right seeds, you are destined for different classes of blessings. There will always be proof of your walk with God:

1. **Family Life** - wealth and riches in his house
2. **Spiritual**- His Righteousness endures forever
3. **Personal** – His Light shines in the darkness; God's grace is evident on his life, and he is full of compassion and humility. He lives and walks with discretion; he's not loud or proud;
4. **Material** - he has so much abundance that he can lend to nations.

When you fear God, you need not fear anything else. The shaking all around you is of no consequence when the inner presence is maintained. Your sustenance is not based on what you have, but in who you know.

When I fear God, I see everything through His eyes. What the world calls evil tidings is God working behind the scenes to perfect everything that concerns me. What gives me this confidence? It is the basis of my trust, the focus of my heart, the One on whom my heart is fixed. If I am fixed on God, I am immovable.

Even those who are my enemies will see and testify that God is with me. How would the world know God if his children do not show Him off? How would the world come to have knowledge of God if those who profess to know him do not live out His life daily?

LESSON FOUR

The Usual and the Unexpected!

And it came to pass in the time of her travail, that, behold, twins were in her womb. And it came to pass, when she travailed, that the one put out his hand: and the midwife took and bound upon his hand a scarlet thread, saying, This came out first. And it came to pass, as he drew back his hand, that, behold, his brother came out: and she said, How hast thou broken forth? This breach be upon thee: therefore his name was called Pharez. And afterward came out his brother, that had the scarlet thread upon his hand: and his name was called Zerah. - Genesis 38:27-30 KJV

Quick Lessons:

1. One of the greatest hindrances to what God can do in our lives is a sense of familiarity and expectation. We see God move in the lives of people close to us; we hear of His acts and workings in the lives of others; we read the accounts of people who experienced God in different ways and then, we come to the conclusion that we know all there is to know about God. We assume that we have explored all options and that God cannot surprise us anymore. Nothing is further from the truth.

2. Just a few years before the above story, the grandfather of these twins had been involved in a similar experience. From birth, he had exhibited signs of supplanting, scheming and slyness. Somehow, he got his birthright through sly means, even though God had already destined to bless him and make him great. He schemed his way through the years until he met the God of destiny, who set him straight and broke the cycle of self-help and self-sufficiency.

3. Fast forward a few years down the line, and we see Jacob's son, Judah, involved in another mess. In fact, this was worse; Jacob tried to outsmart his brother, Judah got involved in prostitution, with his own daughter of all people. Jacob went back to God; Judah went back to his father's house. It matters what you

do when you are confronted with your sin and wrongdoing. When a man grows insensitive to sin, and is unmoved by wrongdoing, that man is on the highway to perdition. When your heart is no longer weighed down by the deceitfulness and false sense of wellbeing that sin promotes, you had better be careful. A person destined for greatness by God may end up in the doldrums of insignificance if s/he does not deal with sin.

4. We see Judah's evil, but we also see God's mercy. We see man's weakness and failures, but we also see God's amazing grace. Who can determine your destiny when God has not determined it? Who can bring to pass any purpose concerning you unless God allows it? Check out the manner of the birth of these twins, and compare this birth to that of Esau and Jacob. Pharez came out first, even though his brother had brought out his arm first. Esau came out first, even though his brother was holding on to his heel. It is not about who comes out first; it is about God's purpose and divine arrangement.

5. Your colleagues may have gone well ahead of you, but being ahead does not necessarily equate to making an impact. Esau came out first, yet is not reckoned with at all today in Israel's history. Zarah put out his hand first, but Pharez came out first, and in the genealogy of Jesus, his name featured. When you are dealing with a God of purpose, your origin,

the circumstances of your birth and your own efforts do not really matter that much. The key factor here is what God says. Jacob spent years scheming and plotting; God was just waiting for Jacob to surrender to him. Pharez was the product of an adulterous, evil relationship, yet he features in the genealogical account of Jesus Himself.

6. People, find your way back to God. You will not amount to much on your own. You were not made to pursue a personal, uncertain agenda; you were created by a God of purpose to fulfill a particular eternal purpose. Read about the accounts of the fathers and mothers of faith, but don't think that God is limited to their own experiences. If you consider that no two have the same experience, God is able to give you a unique experience, something unusual. He has been at work for eternity, fashioning the vessels He will use to fulfill the various dimensions of His eternal purposes. If he can create over 7 billion people, each with a different set of fingerprints, then He can move beyond the usual and give you the breakthrough you need.

7. Don't let your thinking, your past, the stories you have heard or other people's expectations become your focus. God, who had a hand in your birth, irrespective of the circumstances, can move beyond the usual and give you the unexpected. You have to trust Him completely, totally depending on His grace,

power and wisdom. He is the one working on the masterpiece, and He knows just what is required to make the piece turn out perfect. The world can look at you, consider your past and make assumptions and draw conclusions about you. However, know this: if God has not determined your case, nobody can. If God has not finished His work in and on you, people will never understand what they see in you. Why listen to popular opinion if it does not line up with God's opinion? Check your focus; make amendments if you have to. How you see is as important as what you see. Do you see the usual? Are you expecting the unusual, the unexpected and the miraculous? Go back to God.

LESSON FIVE

Getting it Right!

For mine Angel shall go before thee, and bring thee in unto the Amorites, and the Hittites, and the Perizzites, and the Canaanites, the Hivites, and the Jebusites: and I will cut them off. Thou shalt not bow down to their gods, nor serve them, nor do after their works: but thou shalt utterly overthrow them, and quite break down their images. And ye shall serve the Lord your God, and he shall bless thy bread, and thy water; and I will take sickness away from the midst of thee. There shall nothing cast their young, nor be barren, in

thy land: the number of thy days I will fulfil. I will send my fear before thee, and will destroy all the people to whom thou shalt come, and I will make all thine enemies turn their backs unto thee. And I will send hornets before thee, which shall drive out the Hivite, the Canaanite, and the Hittite, from before thee. I will not drive them out from before thee in one year; lest the land become desolate, and the beast of the field multiply against thee. By little and little I will drive them out from before thee, until thou be increased, and inherit the land. And I will set thy bounds from the Red Sea even unto the sea of the Philistines, and from the desert unto the river: for I will deliver the inhabitants of the land into your hand; and thou shalt drive them out before thee. Thou shalt make no covenant with them, nor with their gods. They shall not dwell in thy land, lest they make thee sin against me: for if thou serve their gods, it will surely be a snare unto thee. - Exodus 23:23-33 KJV

Quick Lessons:

1. As has always been established, God's purposes and plans are eternal in origin, scope and effect. There's nothing He is doing now that has not been planned for from the beginning of time itself. Recall that Abraham, long before he even had a son, had already received the promise of a generation that would be slaves in a foreign land but would be delivered by

a mighty hand and given a good land as an inheritance. Fast forward over 700 years; this extract is the point of fulfillment of God's promises. Who says that God ever forgets His promises? Who says God cannot bring His eternal plans to pass, even without our help or input? The first lesson here is central to all that will follow: God is a God of possibilities; a covenant-keeping God who never forgets what He says. He's always at work, working in the now with what He said in the past, and guaranteeing that the future will be exactly as He said.

2. Without God, nothing will work. Ability, capacity and capability only make sense when I am conscious of my need for God. I must settle that fact early on in my life, that God's presence is non-negotiable. It is central to my life, my living and the assignment.

3. You cannot serve God and other gods. It is not possible. The world may teach multitasking and playing it safe, but indeed, God cannot compete for attention with anything in your heart. That is why faith and worry cannot coexist in the same heart. They are parallel lines leading to different eternal destinations. You have to make a choice about who you will follow.

4. You cannot claim God's promises without fulfilling the preconditions. We have become lazy, careless Christians; we have been taught

to demand our rights from God, but nobody seems to teach us our duties as Christians. Even as citizens of a country, can you demand social services without paying your taxes? Can you demand attention from a government to which you pay no dues or owe an allegiance? It is the same in spiritual matters. God has immeasurable blessings, but there are conditions for all these blessings. You will not read any blessing from God that exists without an action/behavior/attitude expected from us, which will activate the blessings. Find a balance.

Check out the blessings promised, and you will find out that they address all facets of life: the physical, the emotional, the psychological, the spiritual and the relational. All facets are covered. That is God – with a plan for all of your life, not just a part of it.

5. Sometimes, God's "slow" process is for our own good. We want things as soon as possible, but we forget that God's wisdom and timing is always on point, working out what is perfect in our lives. We want Him to come now, just like Mary and Martha, but we forget that a greater glory lies just ahead. We want Him to just rise and speak to our problems and make them disappear, just like Naaman, but sometimes, the greatest lessons are learnt in the processes leading to the miracle.

6. The above passage ends with a strong warning: "thou shalt make no covenant with

them, nor with their gods. They shall not dwell in thy land, lest they make thee sin against me, for if thou serve their gods, it will surely be a snare unto thee." The same warning rings throughout our eternal walk with God, and as explained in this book: you are different, you come from different stock, you answer to a different God, you live differently, you love differently, you speak and relate differently. You do not become unequally yoked to people who do not have the kind of Godly fear you have; otherwise they may lead you astray. The power of evil influences is seen in this way: break 20 good eggs into a bowl, then add one bad egg into the mix. No matter how many more good eggs you add, that one bad egg will run through the mix and destroy it all. That is the power of subtle evil influences. When you look at the fall of man, that lesson is so central. All it took was for one person to believe a modified truth from God and for the devil to present it as a lie to man. We have been living with the consequences of that action till now. A good run is better than a bad stand. Avoid evil influences. Run away from sin. Your eternal destination depends on your decisions today.

Now you have heard, you are without excuse. May the Lord help us make the right decisions, seek Him out and walk with Him down here until we translate into eternity.

<u>Call to Personal Relationship with God</u>

For all who realise their need of a Saviour, or who were once saved but had gone back to sinful ways, but now realise that they need to retrace their steps, the prayer below is for you:

Lord Jesus, I come to you today. I realise that I am a sinner, and I cannot save myself. I realise that your death on the cross was for my sins, and your resurrection secures eternal life for all who come to you and put their total trust in you. I also realise that nobody else can save me from the consequences of my sin, which is eternal death.

I come to you today, confessing all my sins to you. I am sorry for all I have done in the past, and I trust in your blood to wash me clean, and secure eternal life for me. I trust in your power to help me live a life free of sin. I depend on your Holy Spirit to help me grow in my knowledge and experience of you, so that whenever this physical life ends, I will reign with you in heaven. Thank you for saving me. In Jesus' name I pray. Amen.

Welcome to the family of God.

9 781838 098810